PIANO ALL THE WAY

(Level Four)

Foreword

level Four of **PIANO ALL THE WAY** introduces the
following concepts in

THEORY:

1. Voices.

2. Chord Inversions.

3. Tonic, Sub-Dominant and Dominant Chords.

4. Cadences: Plagal, Authentic and Complete.

5. Sixteenth notes in quarter time.

6. Compound meters using the eighth note as
   the unit of pulse.

TECHNIC:

1. Voicing.

2. Rolled chords.

3. Melody and accent pedaling.

4. Chromatic fingering.

5. Velocity.

INTERPRETATION:

1. Voicing.

2. Flexibility in timing.

3. Further style variety.

Unit 1
VOICES

Piano music is sometimes written to imitate the voices in a choir.
In the following example, connect the notes of each voice with different color pencils.

The highest note is the Soprano Voice.
The next note down is the Alto Voice.

The next note down is the Tenor Voice.
The lowest note is the Bass Voice.

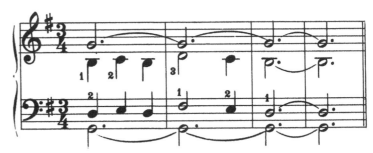

Sometimes one or more of the voices move while the others hold a tone.

Therefore, each note must have a stem of its own to show its time value.

In the following example, which voices move?

Play and count each voice separately.

Play all the voices together.

Stems going up and down from the same note show us that two voices are singing the same tone.
You will find this in the first measure of the chorale below.

CHORALE

SLUMBER SONG

Check the measures where you find special voicing.

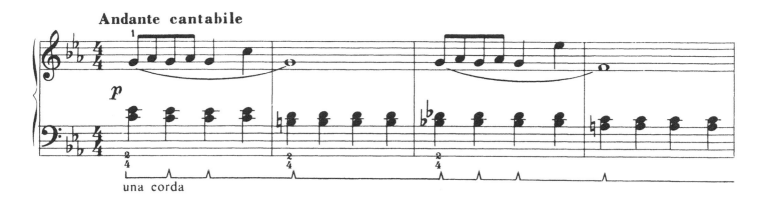

INTERMEZZO

Unit 2

CHORD INVERSIONS

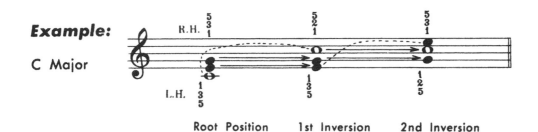

All 3-note chords may be played in 3 different positions.

Example:

C Major

Root Position   1st Inversion   2nd Inversion

Underline the answer:

1. In Root Position, the root tone is the (lowest, middle, highest).
2. In the 1st inversion, the root tone is the (lowest, middle, highest).
3. In the 2nd inversion, the root tone is the (lowest, middle, highest).

Chord Fingering

1. Which two fingers are always used in the chords above? ____ and ____.
2. Explain why the 2nd finger is used in one R.H. position and one L.H. position.

Invert the following Chords on the Keyboard; then write the Notes and Fingering:

a) F Major

b) G Major

c) D Minor

d) E Minor

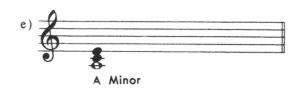

e) A Minor

Identify these chords by name and inversion in the following piece, OLD PLANTATION.

OLD PLANTATION

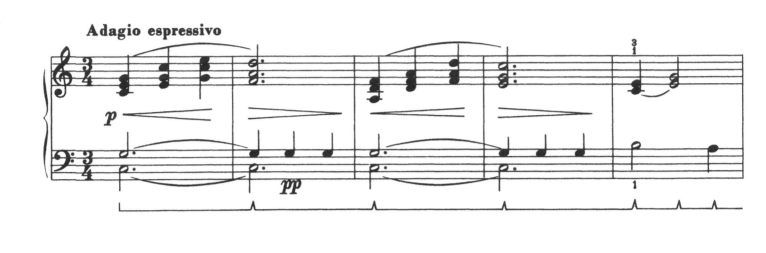

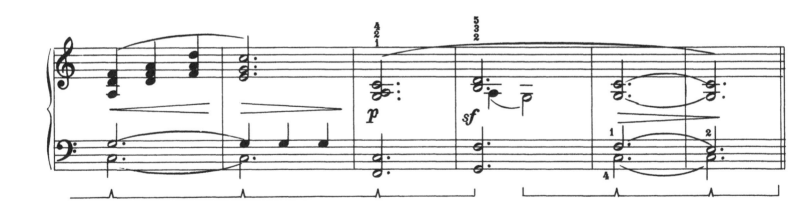

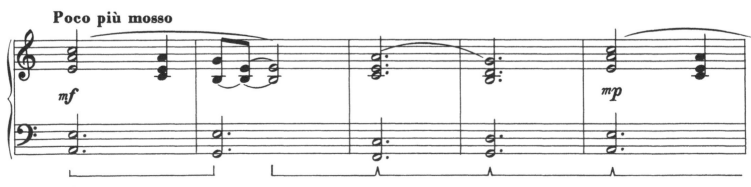

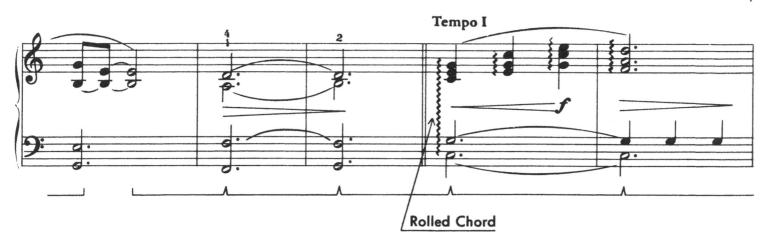

Rolled Chord

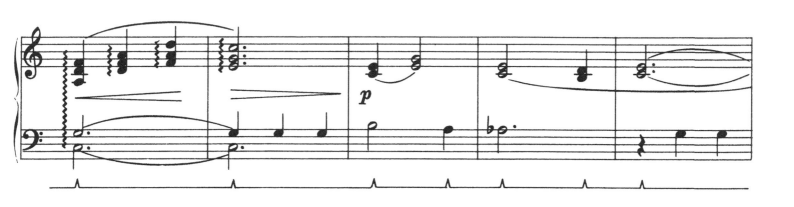

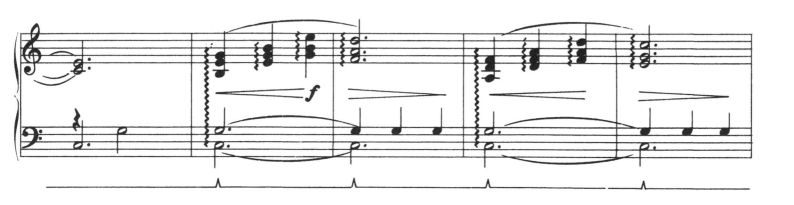

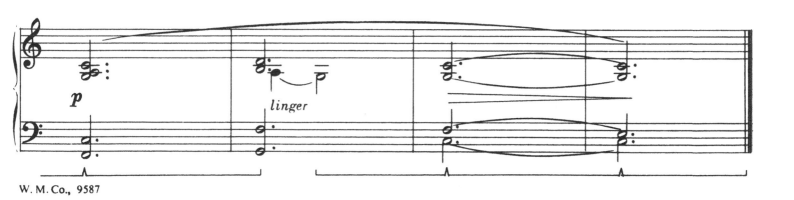

AT THE OPERA

Largo (slowly, broadly)

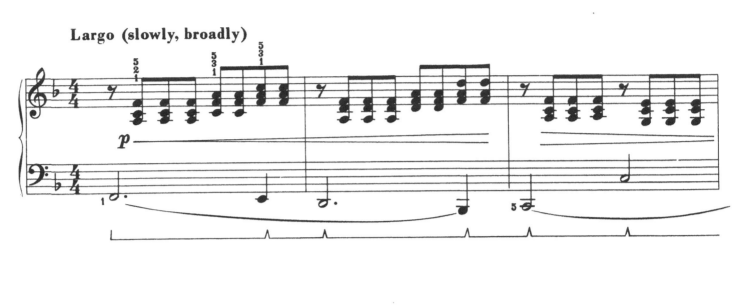

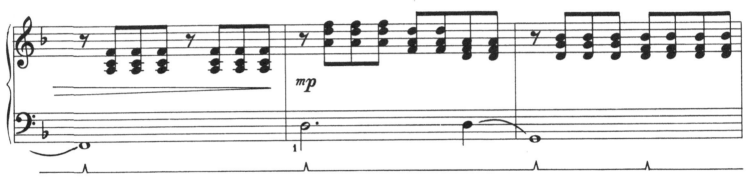

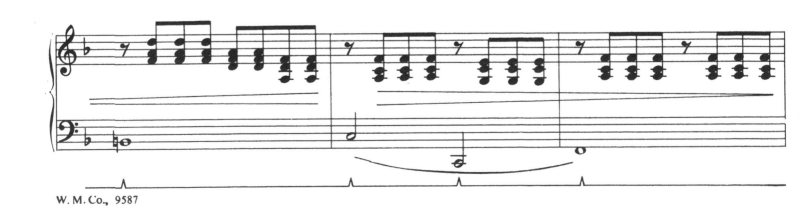

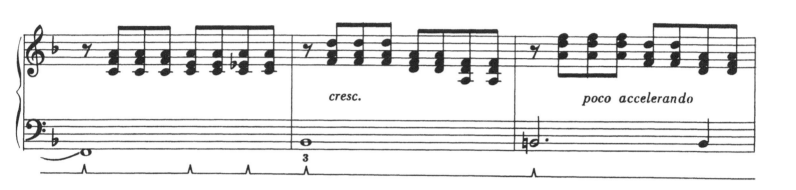

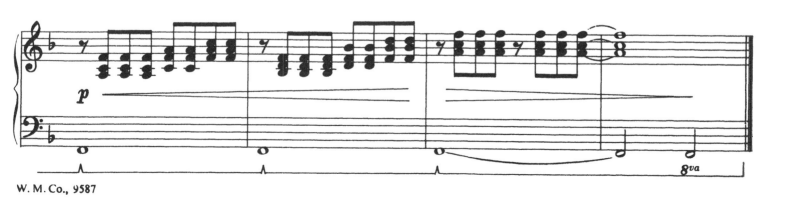

IN OLD VIENNA

Tempo di valse Viennese

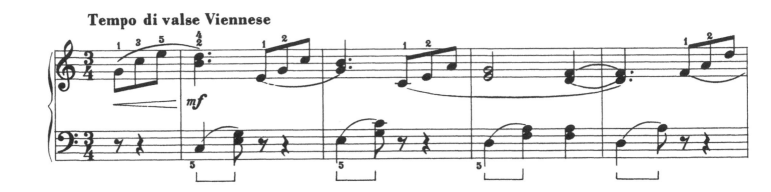

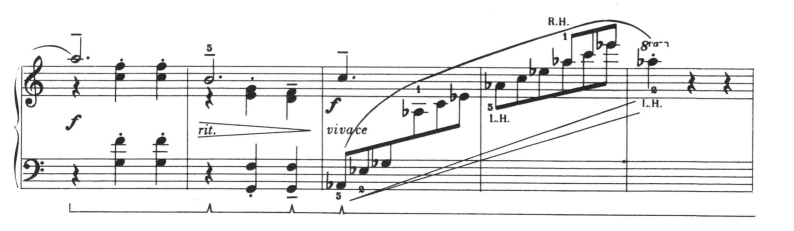

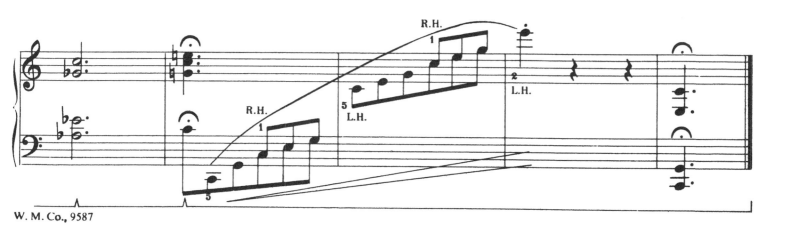

CAPRICCIETTO*

*A small whimsical composition without specific form.

Do the notes in the dotted enclosures form a chord you know?

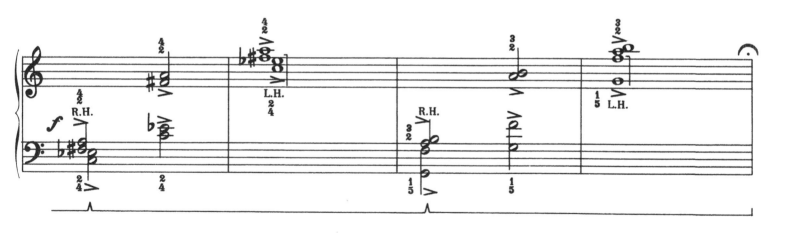

PROJECT: Memorize all MAJOR and MINOR CHORDS in parallel sequence.

Part I

AUGMENTED CHORDS

All major chords become augmented chords when the top note in root position is raised a half tone.

DIMINISHED CHORDS

All minor chords become diminished chords when the top note in root position is lowered a half tone.

Part II

F MAJOR   f minor

Bb MAJOR   bb minor

Eb MAJOR   eb minor

Ab MAJOR   ab minor
              Sounds the same as g# minor

Db MAJCR   db minor
Sounds the same as C# MAJOR   Sounds the same as c# minor

Gb MAJOR   gb minor
Sounds the same as F# MAJOR   Sounds the same as f# minor

Cb MAJOR   cb minor
Sounds the same as B MAJOR   Sounds the same as b minor

*A double-flat (bb) sign is used to lower a note a whole tone.

W. M. Co., 9587

BARCAROLLE*

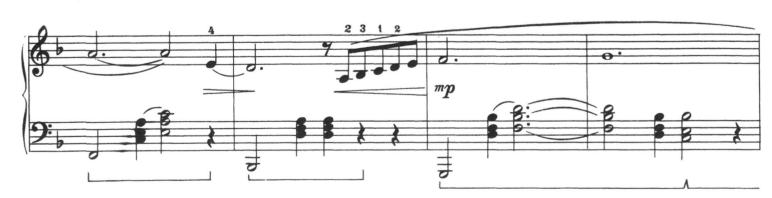

*A boat song in the style of those of the Venetian gondoliers.

W. M. Co., 9587

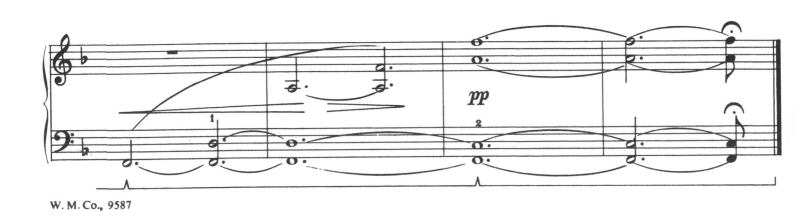

Unit 3

THE TONIC CHORD (I)
THE SUB-DOMINANT CHORD (IV)
THE DOMINANT CHORD (V)

> There are three important chords in each key which are triads built on the TONIC, the SUB-DOMINANT and the DOMINANT tones of the scale.
>
> The root tone of the TONIC CHORD is the first tone of the scale.
> The root tone of the SUB-DOMINANT CHORD is the fourth tone of the scale.
> The root tone of the DOMINANT CHORD is the fifth tone of the scale.
>
> This is the reason these chords are usually identified with
> ROMAN NUMERALS I - IV - V

Example:

KEY OF C MAJOR

Complete the I - IV - V Chords in the following Keys:

Key of F Major

Key of G Major

Key of C Minor (Harmonic Form)

Is there anything unusual about the V chord in the Harmonic Form of the minor scale?

W. M. Co.. 9587

CADENCES

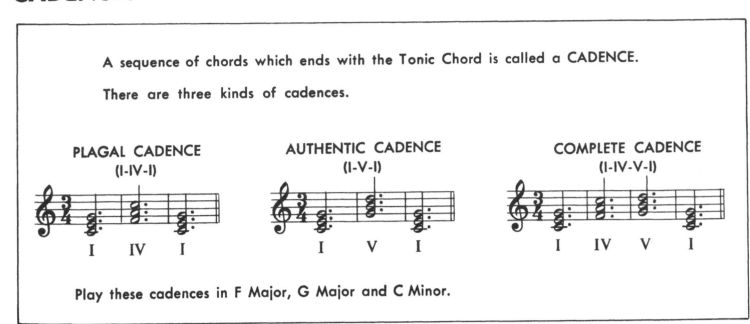

A sequence of chords which ends with the Tonic Chord is called a CADENCE.

There are three kinds of cadences.

PLAGAL CADENCE
(I-IV-I)

I   IV   I

AUTHENTIC CADENCE
(I-V-I)

I   V   I

COMPLETE CADENCE
(I-IV-V-I)

I   IV   V   I

Play these cadences in F Major, G Major and C Minor.

Complete Cadences Using Chord Inversions

Key of C Major

Key of C Minor

Key of F Major

Key of G Major

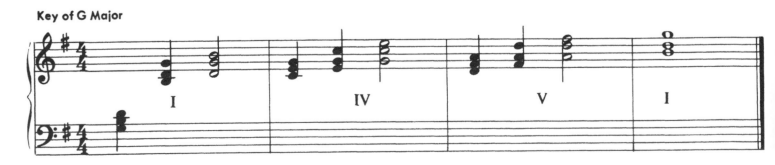

*Which inversion of the TONIC CHORD is used to complete each cadence?

CHORD PRELUDE

Identify all cadences in this piece.

From now on, identify all cadences in your pieces.

VALSE TRISTE

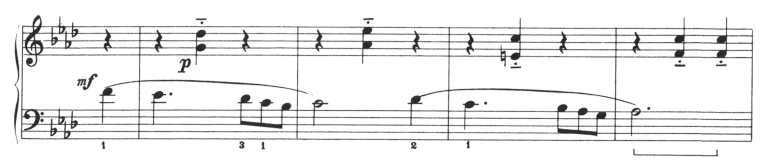

Unit 4

SIXTEENTH NOTES

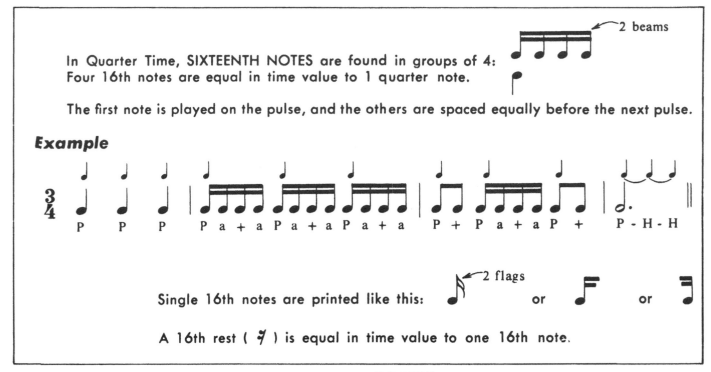

In Quarter Time, SIXTEENTH NOTES are found in groups of 4:
Four 16th notes are equal in time value to 1 quarter note.

The first note is played on the pulse, and the others are spaced equally before the next pulse.

Example

Single 16th notes are printed like this: or   or

A 16th rest ( ) is equal in time value to one 16th note.

RHYTHM READINESS

Write the Pulses (P), the Holds (H), the Ands (+), and the "a"s (a — pronounce "ah").
Then tap and count with the metronome set at 72 for 1 pulse

a) Example:

PETITE ETUDE

AT THE BALLET

CHROMATIC FINGERING

LITTLE WHIRLWIND

Allegro vivace

D.C. al Coda

Variant:

ETUDE
(IN THE STYLE OF CZERNY)

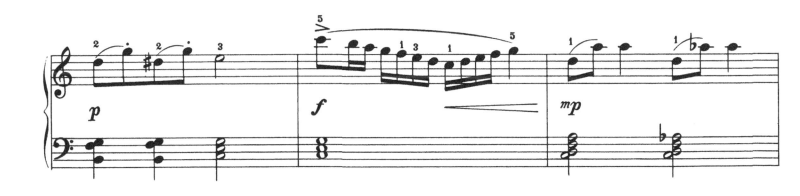

32

Variant:

P a + a

HORSEBACK RIDE

Spiritoso

Variant:

PIECE IN CLASSIC STYLE

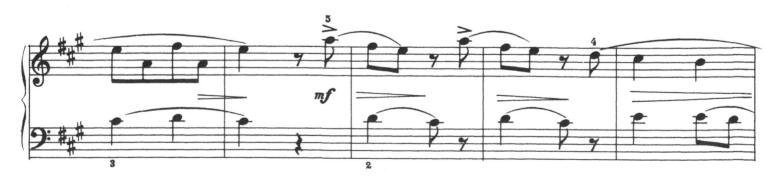

W. M. Co., 9587

Variant:

FIESTA

D.C. al Fine

THE JUGGLER

To Coda ⊕

Unit 5

THE EIGHTH NOTE AS A UNIT OF PULSE

In time signatures where the bottom number is 8, such as

$\frac{3}{8}$ or $\frac{6}{8}$ or $\frac{9}{8}$ or $\frac{12}{8}$ } each ♪ or 𝄾 receives one pulse,

AND ALL OTHER NOTES AND RESTS ARE WORTH TWICE AS MUCH TIME VALUE AS IN QUARTER TIME.

Explain the following:

$\frac{6}{8}$ —→ How many pulses in each measure? _____
—→ What kind of note receives 1 pulse? _____

$\frac{12}{8}$ —→ How many pulses in each measure? _____
—→ What kind of note receives 1 pulse? _____

RHYTHM READINESS

Write the Pulses (P), the Holds (H) and the Ands (+).
Then tap and count with the metronome set at 72 for 1 pulse.

a) Example:

ARABIAN NIGHTS

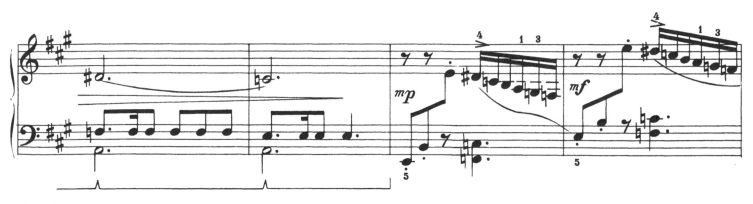

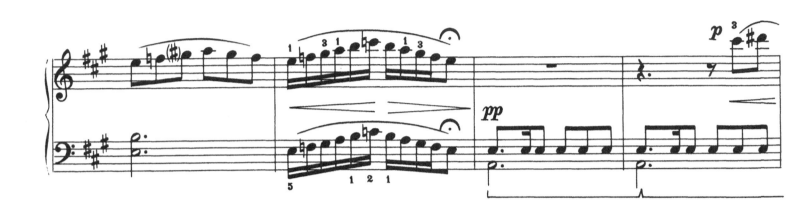

When the tempo is fast, only two pulses to a measure are felt in $\frac{6}{8}$ time. In this case, it is easier to count each group of 3 eighth notes as you would count a triplet in $\frac{2}{4}$ time.

Example:

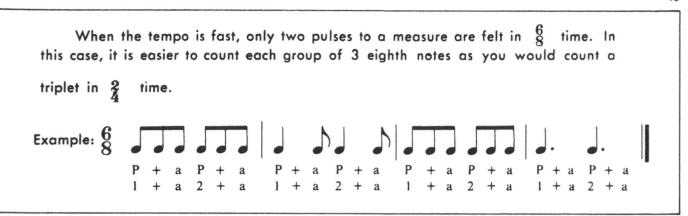

P + a P + a   P + a P + a   P + a P + a   P + a P + a
1 + a 2 + a   1 + a 2 + a   1 + a 2 + a   1 + a 2 + a

While your teacher plays the following piece, tap where you feel the pulses. Play and count the piece, yourself.

POP GOES THE WEASEL

TARANTELLA

W. M. Co., 9587

JOURNEY IN THE NIGHT

Allegro con brio (with vigor)

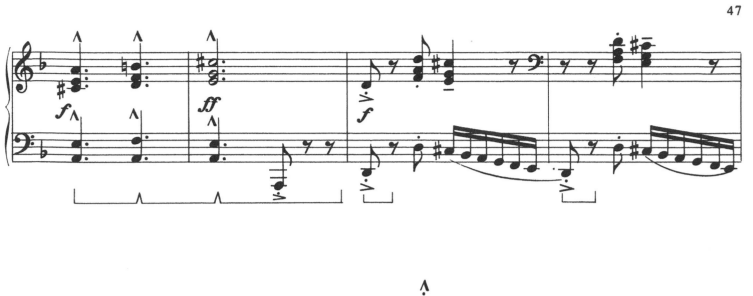

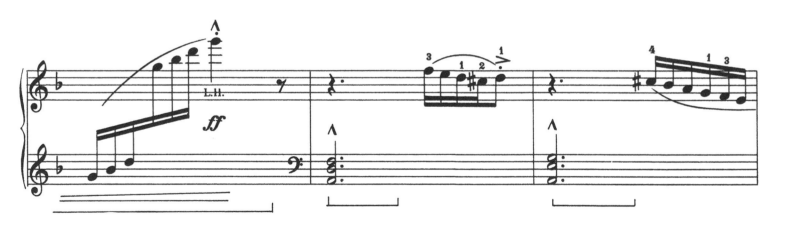

SPANISH ROSES